THE
SLEEP
HOTEL

THE SLEEP HOTEL

AMY NEWLOVE SCHROEDER

Oberlin College Press
Oberlin, Ohio

The FIELD Poetry Series, vol. 25
Oberlin College Press, 50 N. Professor Street, Oberlin, OH 44074
www.oberlin.edu/ocpress

Cover and book design: Steve Farkas
Cover art: Danielle Eubank, *Venice IV* (2007), oil on linen, 18 x 28 inches,
© Danielle Eubank, www.danielleeubank.com

Library of Congress Cataloging-in-Publication Data

Schroeder, Amy Newlove.
  The sleep hotel / Amy Newlove Schroeder.
    p. cm. — (The FIELD poetry series ; v. 25)
  ISBN-13: 978-0-932440-39-6 (pbk. : alk. paper)
  ISBN-10: 0-932440-39-8 (pbk. : alk. paper)
  I. Title
  PS3619.C4646S55 2010
  811'.6—dc22
                                2010001711

for all my teachers
and for Eli

Contents

One

Out in the world, no one sleeps.

—*Federico García Lorca*

One Night Lions Came into My Yard

two females, outlined in black marker
two cubs

I was lying in my white gown
sweat under my breasts
hand between my legs

one male with his lazy mouth

the lions circled the lawn, their huge heads
wheat-colored, even in moonlight:

the grasses of my education—staves—
bent so easily
           under their feet

Rich in Flint

Julia and I drove north
all day to look at leaves

The trees were red with fall's flame-change
The trees were orange

In Vermont a doe's body hung in a tree
draining

A guy in camouflage hosed down his truck
Julia said *you can tell it's real live free or die up here*

Inside me—
                  hot/cold translation of fever

The slain doe leaked from the tree
while the sane face of the sun

retreated behind red-orange leaves

This Far & No Farther

From the plane I saw how the forest was burning
disorganized orange hem

low tide on the mountains

lady next to me *I hate to fly don't you*

Later we flew over clouds
which look like snow if you don't squint

I drank my red drink with limes & no ice
I got drunk

The plane flew east
the sun backed away like an animal

Chalky faces of the other passengers
numb no-self of being with strangers . . .

in the past the hills keep burning

Storytelling

Paper people in a paper land,
a paper house, crazily slanted,
a house like a child would draw:

a square, a triangle, a circle
for the sun.

Stick people stand outside the house
grinning in crayon. No hair, no hands.

Fire people.
But how will you hold the people
when they're burning up in your hand?

Homesick

1.
Her mother misusing the word *elegiac*;
her father calling himself *stupid*—
She runs a tongue over her teeth, thinking
anchorite, cenobite, bite down—

The dog on the lawn, humping his pillow.
The back yard: eugenias and junipers,
browning fescue. Avocados,
azaleas dying in-to-out,
eight star sky.

Flower arranging—a large spiky blue flower
no one knew the name of, looked like a peacock,

The house, the house, the house.

2.
John the Baptist ate bugs, she says
to no one in particular.
Locusts, I think.

She was one of, and her sister beside,
giggling in and out. Breathing.

Someone slips on the mossy bricks. Someone laughs.
Someone blows out the candles, turns on the Jacuzzi,
models the new clothes. Someone covers her mouth.

Way back then, when we used to fight, she thinks, *at least then we…*

Dessert. Desert. Be certain.

When I Used to Go Everywhere with You

the sheep were matted with shit, their wool yellow
they ran when we approached

the goat had an infected eye
clotted with green mucous

I leaned over the chest-high stall to pet the pygmy horses
they huddled close as children

it was hot & the zoo smelled bad

one rooster & a clutch of pissy hens in a wire coop
a three-legged dog slept by the door

you said *someone should really take care of all this*

overhead clouds thickened like yeast

Home Front

The half-life of houses begins:

USA   USA   USA !!!

spray painted
on the cracked macadam.

A dry branch blows past
empty paper bag some newspaper

I thought of us a
man a woman a man

On the next block two Mexican guys
their sweatshirts covered with grime
feed wood into a machine
comes out dust

My hands are numb

Well I did have friends & I

loved them

Pacific

the water is so impersonal,
a stranger to everyone

a child-wind spends itself in the palm
the moon makes endless promises

tonight she's wearing her sailor face,
preparing to cast off

After Reading Lao Tzu

The one who speaks does not know.
The one who knows does not speak,

wrote the old master, which perhaps describes
the situation. Meaning we were all sad.

Meaning that when you were seized by desire,
it was nothing more than flesh, bared above the collarbone

she poured the long night of herself
into empty coffee cans and cornfields

and brushed by air. Meaning: It's chemical. So
that when the moon rears its parched head,

her eyes a mask on her face, the livestock snorting and pacing,
her absent husband . . . she died young

when you feel a finger grazing your neck,
it's only wind created by the movement of

her daughter crying and lighting
fires under the bed

your own body. Downdraft. Live
stock. Because sadness is multiplied

don't worry, she told me,
you can't inherit this

by sadness. A cradle of no compare.
Loose conspiracy of mind and body,

dough swelling over the edge of the bowl,
the yeasty smell of it, a disease that is

a blanket over the window
a pillow over the face

known and not spoken and
also the other one,

who speaks and does not know
what to say.

Q & A

What is the nature of the disease?
Crabgrass and carpenter ants. A funnel.

What is the funnel?
Grape cluster. Echo. Voicebox.

Who hears the echo?
Foxes in the yard. Chickens in the coop.

What do foxes want?
Banditry and hocus pocus.

What's hocus pocus?
Heaven for amateurs.

Where is heaven?
In my mouth. Mouth. A paper spill.

What spills?
Tree blight.

What is blighted?
Politics and the bristly lung case?

What makes you bristle?
Hole-in-corner reasoning. Carnal subtraction.

What was subtracted?
Mayflies. Mysteries. Mathematics.

What is inside mathematics?
Fish eyes & soda balm. Some honest injuns.

What is honesty?
The nature of the disease.

The Clown & the Frog See Everything

striped hat

was that an object from your life?

your life which felt dirempt from objects

the juggler, the fire-eater
the sword-swallower

the trapeze artist befriending the air

you've seen them
moving like insects in the circle of light, performers

hard work in the mouth of the

your granular existence, your circus tent

your new hat

Redeemer Apple

Satellite up, satellite down,
catastrophe circle. The air revolves, cool and dry,
      in the dark of the will.

Skin catalyst. Eye
rotates inside the eye of the flower,
inside the eye of the star,
which explodes like a star.

After stars cross—a bright bouquet—
they quit breathing. Stop.

Who sang star? Who sang satellite?

A purple plum, ringed with apples.
I was alone. Cold air foxed inside my chest.

Where were you, redeemer? I waited for you,
filled my own balloon.

Sonic

where houses used to be

now /
      flight vapor

*

trying to see with the mind
or *through* the mind:

a lot of sex with him—no radiation

(if I didn't love him
he couldn't hurt me)

the streets became empty fields, but still have names like Buena Vista

doesn't air speak
the same fluent language as water?

*

behind the fields, just ocean
trammeled blue canvas, furled god liquid

water a process like being cured,
like watching birds learn to fly

I thought if I could just keep pushing
then something
                  would lift over

the empty fields where my mother's house used to be

*

the thing about sex is that it's rectilinear

       (maybe the house floats in the air like an ark)

I parked behind a couple who were kissing

when the planes go over
it feels like drowning

he said *I've never been on a plane what does it feel like to fly*

I said *kind of metaphorical*

*

at first I was prepared to love him, to love *over* him

a change in air pressure

his cock everywhere inside, a theory of love

so that the air could fill with sand

*

sand-bird, ash-bird

the doves were the color of ash
& there were two of them
in the yoked limbs of the sycamore

picture of myself at 3 & he said *you still look* just *like that, exactly*
   the same

                    —preserved in ash & sand

*

but the truth was I liked being alone

sex with myself so much better—

like   sleepwalking

*

watched the birds fuck in the tree it seemed violent as opera

but I knew better
or thought that I knew better

it looked like battle
wing over tussled wing & a sound like newspaper being torn

people kept asking me—aren't you *married* yet?

*

sweet disinclination

house after house torn down for flight

error in logic:

I didn't love him

                                but the air was hard to breathe

*

the same birds sing over & over from the tree
in daylight I watch them

the male with pepper spots over his feathers

            but it used to be so much *easier*

the female, smaller, no markings, on the branch below

they make a sound like

see-ew—see-ew

*

almost asleep but the birds are peevish

the birds don't sleep
even under the drape of darkness

birdsong, not like bells but bell-shaped

I just wanted to see around it,
around the possibility of flight

chain link fence
diamond-shaped empty

O sound

        hidden in the sea

Caution

Little boys release a fleet of balls at the top of a hill.

The balls, which are red or blue or striped,
run together or apart,
a little population, in the usual flight of populations,
skidding, then bumping down the street.

The balls run down the hill & vanish.
Some are found by dogs. Others are not.

Longing—

It's beautiful

colored lanterns strung on a line

Settled perfectly inside me—
$$\text{the } not \text{ space}$$

where you used to be,
talking to me, extending your hand

Sailboats asleep in their slips

A mechanical sun rises as if pulled by string

Ignis Fatuus

Small flames light up the marsh
I want to eat them

Falseness flames inside me

I love you the way the ground loves the flame

The stars in their distant abstraction
tiny lanterns of desperation

Every night issues new orders, new rules

Small fires mount on the horizon
Their heat is not real, except in the mind

which burns, which is why love ends

The world we could not wait to eat
begins to consume us

Right

I

My friend hisses:
"No one thing can be all things to one person,"
and then looks over at me,
sideways.

I say, "Well, I never thought it would be *all*—"

II

That you wanted to be left alone,
that you wanted to feel part of something—

How weak you are, limp leaf on a clematis vine,
caught always with your sour face and sore wrist.
A writer.

III

The girl reclines. She leans, lee of the stone, *la la la,*
lean-to shack built up against the lie of the house.
Tar paper and cut-bits of cardboard: Ketchup. Green Beans.
Toilet paper.

She thinks she is better than everyone else. She may be right.

IV

The frog leaps out of water; the water falls back on itself.

Night with Echoes

tonight the moon calls
but I only see you,

the blade of your body

like light caught in a paper spill

my courage: water gone to the sea

but your courage is explicit
dark pattern on a red handkerchief

your hair tied up against the rain

2

when I touch you
(I want to touch you)

little pools of water collect at low tide

anemones like asters
the needled bodies of sea urchins

now, later—high tide—

I reach for you

atonal waves hasten me to the shore

3

in the bar I watched you

you watched others

the eyes of the fox
above the field of wheat

I wish that you would look at me

little fox

4

longing shames me

the tulip carves a groove in the air
the linear green stem, like the geometer's drawing

your body & my body
tulips in a jar, or loosely tied with cord

tulips flattered by air

together, but indifferent

they lean their prayerful heads

aspects of meaning

5

night comes for me
even when I can't sleep

I open the window to let you in

listen to the owl
she hunts the darkness

ao I hunt for you

I call to you
but you do not answer

your eyes—tulips—opened for rain

Hollow

Thicket of:
knew I shouldn't,
but wanted him anyway . . .

~

> *Why are the moth wings brown?*
> *Because the accelerated desire is made or stolen.*
>
> *Why do the crows call at night?*
> *A case can be made for no other recourse.*
>
> *Why does the tree grow upward?*
> *Root silence unforgives.*
>
> *(because there are twin lines of deception)*

~

Traveling separately
and together, two orbits
that won't intersect. A problem for geometry
and men with beards, a problem that

                                        doesn't like solutions

~

slowing down the body's progress through air,
remote thick paper \ unmarked, unpencilled

        when will change come
                        so that the light

        ~

O little campfire self

Waterlights

Paper boat on dark water—

Candle inside the boat
which stands for woman

Let the water stand for man.

Downstream the willow unbraids her green tresses.

The water sings as it moves
The banks are sodden, the reeds clogged with mud

The candle makes a chapel of light.
The water sings words no one understands.

Let the willow stand for the self—

I think of the willow
when I think of you.

I try to be the willow

Her pious hair

Throat of green whispers

The One Who Doesn't Love You Doesn't Matter

Struggling to get out
from under the hood of the world,

I drove through the night cathedral
listening to the murmur of the fog:

not you not you not you

The cars ahead burned into smoke.
Lights were embers.

I crouched inside the white companion

when something tugged me up out of my body,

       & held me over
                scattershot
the road

Broken Open by Pills

I think about you so much

that night we made love, awake in the frank
darkness of four a.m.

You saying over and over *it feels so good*
as if you did not believe it

Telescope of missing you

Resorting to a night of intellect
& high ceremony,

tapping my ashes into an empty bottle of beer

Two

Poems Are Remote & Cunning as Fire

Poems rise the dark out of the dark.
Think don't feel my friend A likes to say.
White bones hiss like leaves inside the tree.

What conveys the ochre light like sand & oil?
A's hair fans out in rags of fire while
roots collapse sideways inside the soil.

Like this, like this, like this: a twist of rope
a half-stitched hem. We talk the way birds
talk, from different trees, blindly spite &

blindly love. *Explain or don't complain*, A's
words will peel or strip the bark from the tree.
Can the words consume the light like fire?

I hate A. Sometimes the light creeps crippled
from the shaft; sometimes it glows like leaves.

The World is Transformed by Rain

after Neruda

Green everywhere! Raucous green
I give myself up to you

but do you want me? I think you may be like my lover,
you only come when you aren't wanted,

you only come when I refuse you.
Now the lawns glow in green fire, and I

read them in translation, brown rewritten in green.
Possibly all love is translation.

I never understand what you say
when you're speaking. You change me,

and I let you, so that the barren hills
ripen with grass and the yellow impertinence

of wildflowers. Has the rain stopped?
The sun is so easy to understand, so constant,

it's easy to think like Augustine: *I understood
and then I believed*. I want the opposite,

the irrational rain, wrath of the angered
gods, rain that drives you

to me, because you love me
the way the rain loves the earth—

erratically, with great fury. I don't love you back,
but I flower under your hand, green as limes.

Watching the Sunset on Peconic Bay, Long Island

Standing behind glass, Paula & I watched
the light checker the bay. It was the armistice
between day & night, when the visible surrenders the tangible.

We stood close, but did not touch
as the sun guided its round boat downward.
The sky was scarved in pink and red and blue.

It was all as usual, the trees consumed
by an apparition of fire: first flame, then dark.
For once, the world's beauty didn't bother me.

The Bone Room

beetles & butterflies mounted behind glass

stuffed birds
a crane with a snake in its mouth

a human skeleton hung on a rod

(the day after a month of bleeding
not feeling empty exactly, more passed over)

concentration loose inside the vise

lizards, spiders, a python propped on a forked stake
little printed cards with names in Latin

wouldn't it be easier to say *you're never going to get what you want*

passing through the cycle of stains
red-brown thoroughfare

ruined stillness
                    perfection

How Wide. How Red. How Canopy.

yesterday G said
perfection is your subject

*

oh smoke   oh plumage   oh holy

          under the wide red canopy of your parents dissolving
          under the opening mouth of your first sexual parting

the tomatoes knotted to their wooden stakes
the scent pungent on your hands rub it off it won't come off won't

     practical living: couldn't write so you went back to the garden

(the garden! be serious. . . .

the bees *are* serious)

no sound & couldn't write so you went back to the garden
                              scene of your first

*

remember the garden where you let him
make love to you or no it was your
idea the grass itchy under your thighs &
a whole sky absolution pressing you down
did you imagine it or did someone look out & see you?

     apology in yr. mouth like feathers in the cat's mouth

primitive mouth & the second   mouth

*

couldn't withdraw your critic: the heart of the matter

a man on horseback. no. a child in a carriage. no. a man on a bi-
cycle. no. a woman washing clothes in a bucket. no. a dog on a
line. no. a child hiding under the stairs. no. a woman with
snake-hair folding her hands in her hands. yes probably. snake-
woman with eyes color of grease.

the critic was clean & inflexible, like a new handbag with a
    golden clasp

you were so reachable & the critic was not

        girl self stretched out, long dark shelf . . .

*

*ugly succulent in the garden, no one remembers its name, approxi-
mately 40 yrs. old & belonged to Aunt Ola, who drank beer when she
couldn't sleep & since you do the same thing everything is inherited in-
cluding the past which your mother says blooms*

oh golden night.   oh heritage dust.   oh rootskin & seedling.

        the earth underneath the earth—not your department

girl voice saying *heaven devil let me out*

an inquiry into containment saying *do you really think
the marguerite daisy wants to live like that in a pot.
root bound so obviously not.*

imprint of the day   imprint of the receding hour   imprint of
the garden father

the critic stood on the roof over the garden, radical judge of all
that she surveyed.
her hair was fire!

look at that woman with cobwebs for eyes how can she see that way?

as a child you used to walk around with a book on your head to
improve
your posture
impostor

*

the woman was really a witch of course,

she stood in the garden exchanging air for air & her terrapin skin
which did not come off.

What foul conjuring is this someone might say but you didn't.
you were trying to understand why,
if you planted the tomatoes so far apart, they grew together anyway?

I'm different, you told her, *I'm different because I'm smart.*

that witch was archetypal—she had bells around her neck &
wrists & pointed nails like thorns. in the background someone
was keening. not really music but more like music than anything
else

not that different (her voice filled with sand) *not that different & not
that smart*

*

scrap: you sent for her & she came. your pony-hour redemption.

*

how wide. how red. how canopy.
how moth. how might. how tangent & curving spire.
how tower. how path. how make. how wolf.
how candy-tongue & religion
nowhere.

sexual book under the bed—you found it & you read it

    your *parents'* book

*

the witch was punctuated & the witch was the critic & the witch
   was you—

even when you were seven you felt it:
you were on the swings & the sun was out after a long
rain & you said to yourself *now I see it's a*
                            box with a golden latch

Covet

birds fly when my neighbor tells them to
whenever she waves her hands

or that's how it seems to me

when I think about her, in my lock box of gravel & sand

my clawed face, my scar
Sycorax cleaving the sprite into the tree

it's a jeweled abandon, isn't it   being mean

so happy for you so happy so so

envy consumes itself

     first the face then the hands the feet

First

driving home, we spoke as usual
as if nothing had happened

delicate cookery
impractical experiment
of flesh entering flesh

outside
tough swollen oleanders
ruffled in the wind
as if in conversation

silent illogical exchange
one poisonous flower
to another

Turning Thirty

it's May

campus ferments in jasmine
petunias breathe out their dry medicine

I wander around

on the street corner men drink malt liquor
make signs with their hands

girls huddle outside buildings, pull up their straps
boys laugh

I think about the picture of the hunter
his body borne by the animals

hares, birds & foxes
the dark missions of trees behind

is that the meaning of fealty?
or of feast?

at the corner an old guy fills his shopping cart with cans

Interstate 5

the hills dusted with purple, dusted with orange

swallows dart in and out of mud hives,
their underpass cities

Saturday night a new lover,
the guided eye of sex flashing open

hypnotic, the red familiar
the red phenomenon

like dark water poured from a jug

now: the long drive home
dust, the usual tumbleweeds, the dry grasses

black cloth flutters on the cattle fence

firemen stand in a stubble field, fully suited, practicing,

starting fires   putting them out

Tight, Slack, Tight

today
clarity at the ridgeline

twin selves joined in the no-haze
as clouds pursue each other over the mountains

the brown gift—the grit of clear-headedness
the double-faced bird

tight white clouds impose their delicacy

the freeway curves left, implacable cement barrier
trash strewn in the spillway

cloud-ready

      surrendered to the claim—not the salute—of reason

from the car window, can you see the snow? I can

Jumble

Someone had turned the air into water

so you went out driving—

Coming around the curve at Zuma, you
felt like pollen carried out into the wind

there you feel free

Harum scarum

A red car cut you off—license plate: ONLYART

a woman at the gas station begged for cigarettes,
her pink sweater mottled the color of old blood,

her cardboard sign instructed:

    until the full moon do nothing

Messengers of Error

guy at the market buys
Pampers and beer at 8 a.m.

woman in a ripped T-shirt
waters her lawn through a chain link fence

kids play soccer
on a traffic median,
a yellow strip of grass

on the radio
oh oh oh oh oh oh I still love you so

ducks cross the freeway on-ramp
cars line up to let them pass

homeless guy by the tracks,
pants down, wiping himself

brown hills brown haze—like recompense—

in hot glassine light

Bride Saddle with Stirrups

Galloping into the noose
wind, under the hole-gathered sky

I hold nothing but the mane

At bird-light we travel, my horse & I
cropping grass, drinking from streams

Sometimes I run beside her
one hand on her smooth flank

Her eyes: brown globes on no axis

I was reared on mare's milk

Thick fermented cloud
that boiled my stomach

My taut skin, mare's skin

Roaming heart & ashes

The Sleep Hotel

lights went back & forth in the near distance

Mars was supposed to be close
but I couldn't find it

while my father slept
I sat, open-eyed, in a green vinyl chair—

watching tubes, monitors, joking nurses
who made the same jokes over and over,
wearing their brisk obedient clothes

when he woke I fed him
ice chips from a plastic spoon

Even People I Loved

Winter break alone in St. Louis

Flat on my bed all day
eating peanuts from a jar

watching images flicker

My car got stuck

Outside the blizzard quickened

Narcosis of snow

Gelid New Year's Eve,
past all nuance

Via Negativa

The light is bankrupt
mid-January pearl

Even at noon only partial sun

Your face dissents,
appears repeatedly in dreams

Last night a bed of arrows, a bed of knives
        the slant edge of you—

Orion triangulated overhead
in the yellow-purple sky

Anxious wind, helpmeet to the branches
The leaves lifted and tossed by the neutral breeze

I drank ecstasy, cup of you

woke depraved

A Sense of Proportion

Once you stumble . . . human nature is on you.
—Virginia Woolf

Pain dull red of old blood

The carousel plays the familiar tune
under the cracked parti-colored roof

Buy a ticket &
you can ride—

*

dirty water spill-filling old gutter water / leaves soda cans plastic
bags trash floating mental / canned memory / cigarette butts /
veil of smoke / hard to breathe

human nature is on you

       sounds in the night gather,
                        are spent

*

said Dr. B *please, if you can, quantify the amount of time you feel bad
in a percentage like 30% bad and 70% good & so forth*

monk notes with a green fountain pen

you're in a funk he said agreeably

on the floor the rug swirled indecent colors
rainbow in an oil slick

he was always very neatly pressed & dressed wearing his tie
   Windsor-knotted

through the window some light,
hard to say what %

*

mind shaken from the body
like water shaken from the hands

the pills were blue or orange or yellow

I took them the way other people take God

something green & white—a capsule—and I remember moving
my arms in the air like I was moving them through something
very soft & dense, like animal hair

but break, my heart, for I must hold my tongue

written—

       written *into*

    the dumb show enters

*

felt vestigial

Roman coins on my eyes

no resistance—no repetition

not the way the water won't commit to the sand
how it always pulls away and comes back

not like love

*

Hear my prayer O Lord, and let my cry come unto thee
Hide not thy face from me in the day when I am in trouble

white god-night
puppet body, limbs on string

For my days are consumed like smoke, and my bones are burned as an
*   hearth*

cheat grass grew everywhere
crowding out the world, dry brown fuel

                                        crowding out the rest of
        the world

My days are like a shadow that declineth; I wither like grass

*

Herons part the stillness
their bodies blue as math

they seem to know how still they are / they seem to know

        how to fish in a dry sea

        there's rue for you and here's some for me

so long, Septimus. Septimus, so long—

Brightness Falls

Then the world ignited.
Bad news everywhere,

everywhere plague. We locked
the doors and hid our faces,

we breathed attar of roses
from vials suspended on thread.

As if beauty could keep us safe.
As if beauty could keep us sane.

Nothing could. Too early
for jacaranda but too late for rain

the moon drove herself up
through the boughs of the pine

like a grinning skull. The phone
rang, but no one answered.

Illuminated windows, brilliant night,
moonlight bright enough to read by

if you could hold a thought long enough
to read. This was grief. Someone said once

just think of the word "God" or "love"
& you'll be fine. But even a single word

was too much when the dust
that hid us blew away. Only sleep,

a childhood sleep filled with dreams
of dangerous objects & the men

who carry them.

Think: Fire

Man is that what he thinks; if he thinks fire, he is fire; if he thinks war, then he will cause war. It all depends merely on that the whole of his imagination becomes an entire sun; i.e. that he wholly imagines what he wills.
                    —Paracelsus

The question is—where does it get me?

      or anyone—

*

Not religion but solemnity:

Floating in my grandmother's pool
under the bitter eucalyptus
watching planes fly overhead

Lately the news is bad—worse actually than bad—
& all I can think about are my dead relatives

I really loved my grandmother Muriel & she really loved me

      Oh, stupid

*

[I am embarrassed by this poem it's a fact]

Gardenias turn brown at the tips when you touch them it's a fact

Today M is digging trenches we're not in love it's a fact

the higher a man climbs the easier it is

it's a fact

*

At her memorial service I was 12
I didn't cry b/c that seemed both dramatic & brave

The planes pass over her house they pass over

I think I would like to sleep peacefully in a burlap sack filled
with leaves

*

Yesterday my friend said *did you hear about the terrible things in
    Sudan*
yes I said

Then we talked about M & how it would be better for me not
to see him anymore & *yes* I said

*

That man in the *Purgatorio* who just sleeps & sleeps—he's too
tired & he doesn't get to go forward until his penance is up

Resistance, like trailing your hand in water as Charon's rowboat
moves forward under the purple-dark & starless sky

*

The little patio where Muriel grew things & with bare feet
would walk out to water

her feet long and beautiful wings

*

In the news—blood, beyond

a loose feeling in my bowels & yes my chest & yes my head

Sense of horror can be conveyed through a tone in the voice or
by saying very dramatically *it was too much for me I can't talk
about it*

Barrel-empty—

> or the split barrel, with the curved spines sticking out
> like a porcupine

*

When I was ten, she took my book (*Jane Eyre*) and threw it in
the bathroom trash

She was tired of being around people who read all the time

In my family this is considered a funny story & is sometimes
told at holiday gatherings

I often tell it myself

My favorite part of *Jane E.* is actually when she is at the Lowood
school & they make her stand on a stool to teach her not to lie &
she loves Helen who dies

I like it because it is very clear who is bad & who is good

They had to break the ice in the basins
to wash their little white faces
in the white cold dawn

*

turning off the news, M said *isn't it enough sometimes just to feel*

corollary action: sunlight burns like fire among the leaves

*

Guilt of the personal
like purposely holding your hand to the iron

says Jung *Equally we have a share in gods & devils, saviours and criminals but it would be absurd to attribute these potentialities of the unconscious to ourselves personally . . .*

I would like to believe this but I think that it is not true

says Jung *at the present time too we are once more experiencing this uprising of the destructive forces of the collective psyche. The result has been mass-murder on an unparalleled scale*

If my grief for my granny after 18 years is not so very much abated what else

Lotus-blossom—take & eat of the lotus & sleep the lovely forgetting

Tender as the stalk bent at the root

*

Grief-bouquet harbored long in my heart

constructed with cardboard & cellotape & little
red drops of candle wax dripped red and greasy over the top of
   the box

She was so unhappy & I loved her so much

(yes once they put her in the hospital & yes did apply shocks to
   her brain)

*

What does it feel like to be in the rain of fire

Pull the veil of leaves over your face & sleep inside the burlap
   sack

Tea with my friends on Friday afternoon looking at the ocean
we talked about death & war & Republicans
we spoke about the compassion problem

Mostly we looked at the sea & everything bad seemed very far
   away from me

*

My other friend said *so what are you going to do / move to Palestine?*

*

We used to go to the nursery together

I loved the greenhouse

the smell of damp soil & the air so wet you were almost breath-
    ing water

I would go into that light closed warm space
to look at the green ribs of the leaves

*

Prostitutes in Delhi, ten or twenty men a day
a little area made out of colored sheets hung on wire

the mind has been here before or
has the mind ever been here before?

*

And I saw issuing from on high, descend
Two angels, each with flaming sword in hand
Broken short off and blunted at the end.
Green as the just-born leaves ere they expand,
Their raiment was, which they behind them trailed,
By the green wings ever disturbed and fanned.

*

Cheatgrass spread everywhere over the rough hills of the
    peninsula

            My heart wasn't in it, but I drove on further

                    to watch planes pass over the jeweled
                    veins of the sea

Prophecy

Light over water
turned it brown,
particulate with sand

gulls fished in the light-rectangle
bobbing heads, down and then back up

I had been thinking about Cassandra

her dream-sorrow

done with feeding
the gulls slept/rocked on the water

distaff of the waves—

or what made us distaff—

The Wake

I could not bring you with me, old self,
carry you in my arms like a stillborn colt,
rickety body slick with membrane.

I wanted to breathe;
you wanted to succeed, or at least go
forward, a tall horse jumping over a wall.

Instead: the morning light that moves
over the wall like the surface of the ocean,
small shadows fingering bricks like anemones.

No one chased me.
Still, I ran like Daphne,
turning and turning into the heart of the tree.

Notes

"The Clown and the Frog See Everything" is the title of a child's dream drawing exhibited at the University Village shopping center in downtown Los Angeles.

"The Bone Room" is the name of a taxidermist's shop in Albany, CA.

"Turning Thirty" refers to "The Hunter's Funeral Procession," which inspired the third movement of Gustav Mahler's First Symphony.

The title "Messengers of Error" is drawn from the gnostic gospel "The Apocalypse of Peter," one of the texts uncovered at Nag Hammadi. The poem also contains a line inspired by the song "D'yer Mak'er" by Led Zeppelin.

The title of "Bride Saddle with Stirrups" refers to a decorative saddle used by nomadic tribes in 10th century Eurasia.

The title of "A Sense of Proportion" comes from Virginia Woolf's *Mrs. Dalloway*. In addition to quotations from Woolf's book, the poem also contains lines from *Hamlet* and from the 102nd Psalm.

The phrase "brightness falls" is drawn from "A Litany in Time of Plague" by Thomas Nashe. The poem also contains a line from *The Cloud of Unknowing*.

In "Think: Fire," the line "the higher a man climbs the easier it is" is from Canto IV of Dante's *Purgatorio*, translated by Dorothy Sayers. The penultimate stanza of the poem is drawn from Canto VIII of the same translation. The quotations from Jung can be found in *Two Essays on Analytic Psychology*.

"Poems Are Remote and Cunning as Fire" is dedicated to Carol Muske-Dukes. "Watching the Sunset on Peconic Bay, Long Island" is for Paula Mauro. "Turning Thirty" is for Brian Kane. "Think: Fire" is dedicated to Muriel Newlove, *in memoriam*.

Acknowledgments

Grateful thanks to the editors of the following journals, in which these poems originally appeared, sometimes in different versions:

American Poetry Review: "Covet," "Home Front," "One Night Lions Came into My Yard," "Watching the Sunset on Peconic Bay, Long Island"

Colorado Review: "Via Negativa"

Eclipse: "After Reading Lao Tzu"

FIELD: "Homesick" and "Right"

La Petite Zine: "The Clown and the Frog See Everything" and "Bride Saddle with Stirrups"

LIT: "Hollow"

Lyric: "Interstate 5," "The One Who Doesn't Love You Doesn't Matter," "This Far and No Farther"

Pleiades: "Poems Are Remote and Cunning as Fire"

Ploughshares: "Waterlights"

POOL: "Brightness Falls," "Ignis Fatuus," "The World is Transformed by Rain"

Seneca Review: "Q & A"

VOLT: "How Wide. How Red. How Canopy."

*

I am grateful to my editors at Oberlin, for their generosity and assistance with the publication of this book. Many, many thanks to Susan McCabe, Carol Muske-Dukes, and David St. John for their counsel, encouragement, and love. I am grateful to the Creative Writing and Literature program at the University of Southern California, which gave me the time and support needed to complete this book. I would like to thank Marjorie Becker, Molly Bendall, Amaranth Borsuk, Elena Karina Byrne, Kate Chandler, Danielle Eubank, the Hamilton family, Julia Hanna, Joy Katz, David Dodd

Lee, Paula Mauro, Carl Phillips, P. B. Rippey, Judith Taylor, and Jean Valentine. Particular thanks to Gretchen Mattox and L. B. Thompson.

My gratitude to my family is immeasurable—thanks for helping me keep the faith. None of it is possible without you.

Thanks also to Chester, wherever you are, wherever you may be.

About the Author

Amy Newlove Schroeder is a fourth-generation California native. A founding editor of *POOL*, her poems and reviews have appeared in *American Poetry Review*, *Boston Review*, *Ploughshares*, *FIELD*, *Seneca Review*, *LIT*, and other journals. She has been educated at UC Berkeley, Washington University in St. Louis, and the University of Southern California, where she completed a doctorate in literature and creative writing. She lives in Istanbul.